**W9-AYP-461**

You may be saying, "This is just what I need. Another dumb book to read, as if my school books weren't enough." If you feel this way, take a look at the next few pages. In no time, you'll see that **Graffiti: Devotions for Guys** deals with practical issues. It gives you biblical advice for your problems, such as conflicts with your parents . . . peer pressure and temptation . . . fear, insecurity, and doubt . . . dating and sex . . . popularity and reputation . . . and loneliness and depression, to mention a few. And this devotional will boost you spiritually by giving you a better understanding of God and His plans and expectations for you. So if you're really interested in the shape you're in—not just spiritually, but physically, socially, mentally, and emotionally as well—then keep reading. You'll find out this isn't just another "dumb book."

# GRAFFITI:
## Devotions for Guys

# GRAFFITI:
## Devotions for Guys

# J. DAVID SCHMIDT

**Power Books**

## FLEMING H. REVELL COMPANY
## OLD TAPPAN, NEW JERSEY

Scripture quotations are taken from:
HOLY BIBLE: NEW INTERNATIONAL VERSION
Copyright © 1978 by the New York
International Bible Society. Used by
permission of Zondervan Bible Publishers.

Excerpt from "Can't Buy Me Love"
(John Lennon and Paul McCartney)
© 1964 Northern Songs Limited
All rights for the U.S.A., Mexico, and the
Philippines controlled by Maclen Music, Inc.
c/o ATV Music Corp.
Used by permission. All rights reserved.

Excerpt from "If" by David Gates:
Copyright © 1971 by Colgems-EMI Music, Inc.
6255 Sunset Blvd., Hollywood, CA 90028.
Used By Permission. All Rights Reserved.

Library of Congress Cataloging in Publication Data

Schmidt, J. David (John David)
    Graffiti: devotions for guys.

    Summary: Fifty-six discussions, each with a relevant Bible verse, on topics such as
dating, parents, popularity, rejection, faith, sexual temptation, and other aspects of
daily life.
    1. Adolescent boys—Prayer-books and devotions—English. [1. Prayer books and
devotions.   2. Christian Life] I. Title.
BV4855.S35    1983          242′.632          83-3191
ISBN 0-8007-5114-0

Copyright © 1983 by J. David Schmidt
Published by Fleming H. Revell Company
All rights reserved
Printed in the United States of America

Thank you,
Mom and Dad,
you're my best friends.

# BEFORE YOU READ

# THIS BOOK

# READ THIS PAGE

You're probably saying at this point, "Here's another one of those dumb devotional books my mother bought me."

But do you know what? Your mom, or whoever bought you this book, just might have finally come through for you.

This is one of those devotional books that doesn't require you to do a homework assignment every time you pick it up. You don't have to make any lists, write any poems, or say any cute prayers. All you have to do is grab your Bible, this book, and maybe a Coke and find a comfortable place to read.

God will do the rest, because this book has been written with you in mind. It doesn't try to give easy answers to some of the big questions in your life.

What it does try to do is help you see that the Bible is not as heavy and complicated as you might think, and also, that it doesn't have to hurt to be a Christian.

Oh, yes, one more thing. For what it's worth to you, I've been where you are. I've fallen asleep lots of times trying to read my Bible, picked up my share of dirty magazines, and felt like a first-class jerk at times too. But I'll tell you something. If you're willing to give Him a shot at it, God can and will help you in your life. I hope as you read this book you'll see what God can do for you.

J. David

# CONTENTS

*Dad's right, wheels aren't everything in life.*
*I mean, after girls, I'd say they rank second.*

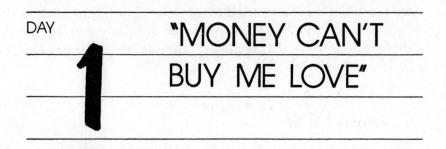

# "MONEY CAN'T BUY ME LOVE"

> Money can't buy me love,
> can't buy me love. . .
>
> LENNON, McCARTNEY

This classic song by the Beatles describes what some guys try to do: buy love and intimacy. It's funny, in a sad way, the places people try to buy love—in the backseat of a car, in a dirty magazine, in a cheap hotel. Since the beginning of time men have tried to buy love and intimacy from women. It can't be done.

**Take a minute to read Proverbs 7, which talks about the consequences of buying love.**

The movies and other media don't tell you about the unwanted babies, lost self-respect, venereal disease, and pain that come from trying to buy love. The Bible says if you want to find the road to hell, look for the people who are buying and selling love. The Bible also says that when you try to buy love, you sin against your own body. The results are worse in many ways than those of other sins.

God has a better idea. It can be summed up in one word—*purity*. Purity is not a state of perfection. It is a state of mind and heart that affects how you behave. It's not just for girls either. It's something God wants you to work toward. If you watch what you read, what movies you go to, and who your friends are, and you ask God to help you *every day* to be pure, you will find that your batting average is going to go up. Purity, which you once thought was unattainable, is reachable, but not if you try to do it through your own strength. You are worth too much to God and yourself to use your money, time, and energy to buy love. As you actively and regularly ask God for strength, you'll find that the heavy pressure on you to buy love will be more manageable.

### Proverbs 7:24–27

Now then, my sons, listen to me; pay attention to what I say. Do not let your heart turn to her ways or stray into her paths. Many are the victims she has brought down; her slain are a mighty throng. Her house is a highway to the grave, leading down to the chambers of death.

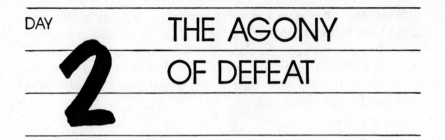

# THE AGONY
# OF DEFEAT

ABC's "Wide World of Sports" has a classic video shot of a skier coming down the ramp, losing it, and crashing through hay bales, people, and piles of snow—"the agony of defeat." If you're into any sport and have lost a game or meet recently, or even if you've been turned down for a date, you know the pain you feel somewhere between your tonsils and your stomach. Defeat is no fun, and it's an inconvenience to anyone who wants to win.

Should winning be important? Are some victories more important than others? Let's look at what the Bible has to say about this subject. **Take a few moments and read 2 Samuel 11.**

On the surface it looked like David was a winner. He not only got away with sleeping with Bathsheba, but he also was able to cover up the plot to have her husband, Uriah, killed. But David blew it. Like we often do, he forgot that God saw what he had done. If you read the next several chapters of 2 Samuel, you will learn that eventually David's sins were exposed and what looked like a victorious cover-up turned into tragedy. David's honor was tarnished, his daughter raped, and his son killed. It was only after all this and David's asking God for forgiveness that there was any "victory" for David.

We should learn from this story that some defeats are more important than others. A good test to see whether a defeat is important or not is to ask yourself, *Will it matter a year from now?* Putting some of the smaller defeats in life into perspective will help you to handle losing.

David really messed up his life for a time. Yet, because his heart was right, God forgave him and built his character in the process. Maybe you've lost some pretty big battles in life. You don't have to live forever with that defeat. Jesus said to come to Him if you are weary (of defeat) and He will give you rest. If you are willing to talk to God and involve Him in your struggles, He will help you turn those defeats into constructive building blocks in your life.

### 2 Samuel 11:2–5

One evening David got up from his bed and walked around on the roof of the palace. From the roof he saw a woman bathing. The woman was very beautiful, and David sent someone to find out about her. The man said, "Isn't this Bathsheba, the daughter of Eliam and the wife of Uriah the Hittite?" Then David sent messengers to get her. She came to him, and he slept with her. (She had purified herself from her uncleanness.) Then she went back home. The woman conceived and sent word to David, saying, "I am pregnant."

# WHO ME, SCARED?

Most fellows would rarely, if ever, admit to being afraid. The stakes are too high. If some of your friends found out that you were afraid of driving alone on back roads at night, or going off the high dive, or asking out that cute girl in Algebra—you're convinced they'd laugh at you till graduation. If you admit, as a guy, that you get afraid sometimes it's, well, it's almost unpatriotic.

Actually, everyone feels fear now and then. Fear of being alone, new situations, losing someone important to you, and other fears are common to all people. God Himself had something to say about fear.

**You can read about God's promise for when you are afraid in Isaiah 41:10-16.** When God created the heavens and Earth, He did it simply by speaking. Can you imagine the ability to create a whole universe just by opening your mouth and saying a few words? In these verses in Isaiah, God is speaking again— this time He's saying, "Fear not, I am with you." If God's words are powerful enough to create the universe, He is certainly powerful enough to back up the promise, "I am your God, I will strengthen you; I will help you." Fear paralyzes us; it makes us panic. If we don't learn to contain it, it can spill over into other areas of our lives. God knew about fear's effect on our minds. That's why He made it very clear that we don't need to fear. God is always present and strong enough to help us—no matter how silly or how significant the fear may be. Next time you fear, ask God to be with you and to help you. You can count on Him.

### Isaiah 41:10, 13

So do not fear, for I am with you; do not be dismayed, for I am your God. I will strengthen you and help you; I will uphold you with my righteous right hand. . . . For I am the Lord, your God, who takes hold of your right hand and says to you, Do not fear; I will help you.

**"God is always present and strong enough to help us. . . ."**

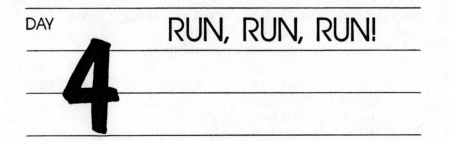

# RUN, RUN, RUN!

Have you ever noticed how often you are bombarded with some type of sex message? Open up a magazine and some slinky chick in a bikini is advertising a soft drink. Or go to the store to pick up a loaf of bread for your mom and across the top of the magazine rack are more dirty magazines than you could read in a week. Our society is saturated with sex. What is the solution if you want to honor God and yourself by working hard at being pure?

There's an interesting account in the Bible about how one young guy handled it long ago. **Take a minute and read Genesis 39.**

There's no doubt about it. Potiphar's wife must have been some fox. How could Joseph not give in? *He ran.* What were the results? In the short run, Joseph probably was frustrated sexually, besides going to prison. But God helped him with both troubles. The Bible says that God was kind to Joseph and gave him success in whatever he did.

What can this mean to you? Sex is one of the most difficult things to handle in life. There is no surefire plan for 100 percent success over every sexual temptation. And at your age, sex is especially difficult to deal with. But God understands you and how difficult this part of your life can be. And He has a way to help you. You can learn from Joseph. He did the smart thing by running, and by asking God to help you, you can learn to run, too.

Don't worry about your past failures to think good thoughts or do or say the right thing. God can and will forgive you if you ask Him. Look to the future and begin today to ask God to help you to run like Joseph did.

Here are four ways you can run from sexual sin:

1. You can't help seeing and appreciating a good-looking girl. *RUN* from spending any time at all thinking sexual thoughts about her.
2. *RUN* by not stopping even to pick up a dirty magazine to leaf through it.
3. *RUN* by turning the TV off when a show that will give you trouble with your thoughts comes on.
4. *RUN* by not rehashing in your mind the comments made by friends whose standards are different than yours.

Joseph ran away from sexual sin. By asking God to help you and doing your part, you can, too.

### Genesis 39:6–12

Now Joseph was well-built and handsome, and after a while his master's wife took notice of Joseph and said, "Come to bed with me!"

But he refused. "With me in charge," he told her, "my master does not concern himself with anything in the house; everything he owns he has entrusted to my care. No one is greater in this house than I am. My master has withheld nothing from me except you, because you are his wife. How then could I do such a wicked thing and sin against God?" And though she spoke to Joseph day after day, he refused to go to bed with her or even be with her.

One day he went into the house to attend to his duties, and none of the household servants was inside. She caught him by his cloak and said, "Come to bed with me!" But he left his cloak in her hand and ran out of the house.

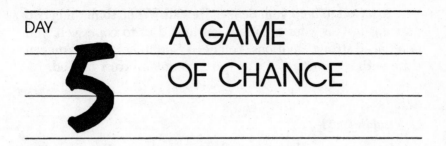

# A GAME
# OF CHANCE

Roll the dice. Pick up a green card. Card says STOP. Your brother dies in a car accident. Turn in all your cards and money. Game over. You lose.

It *can* happen and does. People, sometimes good people, die young, and the world of their families and friends turns to hell. A soccer-player friend of yours goes home one night after practice and hangs himself. Your dad walks out on your mom and family one day for some girl at the office. Your best friend gets a girl pregnant, then pays for her to have an abortion. Your mom dies of cancer. Inside you fall apart. This can't be happening. All you seem to be able to do is ask why.

Coping with the hurt and pain of life will be one of your toughest challenges. How well do you cope? What strength do you draw on? God's Word has some encouragement for you when you hurt. **Take a minute and read Isaiah 40:25–31.**

The last verse is a familiar one. Sometimes familiar verses lose their meaning when they are used lightly. But a closer look at this verse will tell you three things about how to cope when things go wrong in life:

1. We gain strength by waiting. Waiting on God means asking Him to help you, then watching to see how He will do it.
2. This verse is a promise. God never has or never will go back on a promise. But it is up to us to believe it.
3. The strength God gives is to help us to do normal things like running and walking through life as well as to exceed what we thought possible ("fly like an eagle").

Ask God to help you. *Believe* He will. When something bad happens to you, your emotions get hurt. But to cope well, you don't need strong emotions. You need God to help you. You can cope with the hurts of life as you lean on and trust in God.

### Isaiah 40:28–31

Do you know? Have you not heard? The Lord is the everlasting God, the Creator of the ends of the earth. He will not grow tired or weary, and his understanding no one can fathom. He gives strength to the weary and increases the power of the weak. Even youths grow tired and weary and young men stumble and fall; but those who hope in the Lord will renew their strength. They will soar on wings like eagles; they will run and not grow weary; they will walk and not be faint.

# 6 LEADER OR FOLLOWER?

Do you think you have the qualities to be a leader? Well, here's some good news. You don't have to be six-feet-tall, good-looking, dress first-class, or have a rich dad to be a leader. The qualities of leadership are not related to these things. Let's look at what the greatest king of Israel told his son about the qualities of a good leader. **Take some time and read 1 Kings 2:1-4.**

Maybe you're not captain of the swim team, a student government leader, or a youth group president, but the qualities David told his son he needed are qualities you can develop too:

*Strength:*
Stay balanced physically in what you eat and work to stay in shape.

*Be Worthy:*
Command the respect of the guys in your class because of your wisdom and your respect for others.

*Obey God's Laws:*
If you obey the Ten Commandments you'll keep your nose clean and spare yourself a lot of hassles.

*Follow God's Laws:*
When life gets tough, always remember God works things out in life for His honor and your best.

Leaders are made, not born. If you involve God in the process, you too can develop the qualities an experienced old king thought were important enough to recommend to his son.

### 1 Kings 2:1–4

When the time drew near for David to die, he gave a charge to Solomon his son. "I am about to go the way of all the earth," he said. "So be strong, show yourself a man, and observe what the Lord your God requires: Walk in his ways, and keep his decrees and commands, his laws and requirements, as written in the Law of Moses, so that you may prosper in all you do and wherever you go, and that the Lord may keep his promise to me: 'If your descendants watch how they live, and if they walk faithfully before me with all their heart and soul, you will never fail to have a man on the throne of Israel.' "

# GOD'S GAME PLAN

It's happened to all of us. You walk into the locker room after practice, and your friends stop talking and head for the showers. You try to pass it off, but inside you feel alone.

Feeling left out of a group or being alone is about as much fun as going on a ski trip with a parakeet. Throughout your life you'll face times when you will be left out of a group. A sense of rejection and loneliness will set in. You will need help. Where is it?

**Take a minute to read Jeremiah 29:11–13.**

This guy Jeremiah felt discouraged and alone much of his life. God had given him the job of telling the Jewish nation to get its act together—to get back to worshipping God. Jeremiah needed a promise he could live by when he got lonely and one he could share with the Jews.

God's promise came out like this:

1. God has plans for you, for good, not evil. That means you aren't alone, even when you feel alone. Someone smarter and stronger than you is looking out for your best interest.
2. God's plans will give you a future and hope. That doesn't mean hassle-free living. It means whatever happens to you, God will bring good out of it.
3. God hears your prayers. Being part of a group at the time feels important. God knows your hurt or loneliness when that doesn't happen.
4. You can find God if you want to. The way to find Him is simple enough—talk (pray) with Him and look for Him in the friendship of other people.

Loneliness is never fun, but knowing God is there and involved in your life can only take the edge off your loneliness. By taking this promise and putting it to work in your life, you can cut your loneliness in half.

### Jeremiah 29:11-13

"For I know the plans I have for you," declares the Lord, "plans to prosper you and not to harm you, plans to give you hope and a future. Then you will call upon me and come and pray to me, and I will listen to you. You will seek me and find me when you seek me with all your heart."

**❝ ... you aren't alone, even when you feel alone. ❞**

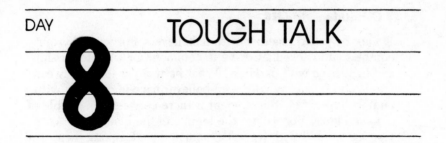

# TOUGH TALK

Here's some tough talk. As much as you may hate it, dating girls who don't personally know God is out—off limits—and no good for you if you're serious about maintaining your walk with God. If you find this really hard to take, you're not alone. Millions of guys before you, around the world and down through the ages, also hated it. Some said, "Hang it," did things their way, and paid the price with broken marriages and a lot of pain.

**Take some time to read what the Bible says about this subject. Read 2 Corinthians 6:14–18.**

"How can one simple date with a non-Christian girl cause any hassle?" "No one falls in love by going to just one football game together." "She needs me to tell her about the Lord."

These kinds of statements are valid to a point. But you still have to come back to what the Bible says. The verses you read don't pull any punches. When it comes to dating and marriage there is no harmony between the believer and unbeliever. Some guys would say their values are the same as the girl's, but the bottom line remains that the Christian's purpose on Earth is to please God, while the non-Christian's is to please herself or another person. You and she are going in two different directions.

This issue separates the men from the boys. If you have a serious relationship with a non-Christian girl, you need to stop and rethink where you are and where you are going with her. If doing the right thing is doing the tough thing, you can count on God to see you through.

### 2 Corinthians 6:14–16

Do not be yoked together with unbelievers. For what do right-eousness and wickedness have in common? Or what fellowship can light have with darkness? What harmony is there between Christ and Belial? What does a believer have in common with an unbeliever? What agreement is there between the temple of God and idols? For we are the temple of the living God. As God has said: "I will live with them and walk among them, and I will be their God, and they will be my people."

# 9 ARE THEY FOR REAL?

Hidden underneath mattresses and locked in bottom bureau drawers across North America are a lot of dirty magazines. Hollywood makes fun of those hidden magazines. But the guys who hid them (and some are Christians) have bought into an illusion about girls. The illusion of pornography is dangerous to you and your concept of girls.

**Take a moment and read 2 Timothy 2:22 to see what it says about this.** This verse readily admits that young men have trouble thinking pure thoughts. One of the problems with dirty magazines is that they aggravate your thought life at a time when it's very difficult to think clean thoughts anyway.

If you could see behind the scenes of the best-selling dirty magazines, you would discover a team of people working over pictures with air brushes. Their job is to remove any spots or blemishes on the pictures which would interfere with the illusion that is being created. The end product is a perfect woman—or so they would like you to believe.

"So what," you could say, "they still are fun to look at." The problem is that *no* girl will ever measure up to the illusion, even the girl in the picture.

A steady diet of dirty pictures leaves you with unrealistic expectations of the imperfect but pretty girls who would come into your life. Adjusting to the difference is very difficult.

The Bible draws a clear distinction. Pornography reduces women to sex objects. The Bible says to enjoy the company of people who love the Lord. Reading dirty magazines is like keeping company with the wrong people.

Are you sleeping on any smut? This is a good time to recognize its effect on your life and make a trip to the garbage can. With God's help (if you call on Him), you can avoid the pornography illusion in the future.

### 2 Timothy 2:22

Flee the evil desires of youth, and pursue righteousness, faith, love and peace, along with those who call on the Lord out of a pure heart.

*Oh brother, some things never seem to change!*

# 10     MACHO MAN

Respect is not something that will ever be just handed to you in life. It is something you will have to earn. As a man, you not only need to have self-respect but you need to have the respect of those around you, especially women. Some fellows have their own ideas of how to be respected by women. God has a different idea. **Take some time right now to read Philippians 2:3–11.**

Some guys would say you earn the respect of women by

—being macho
—being sexually aggressive
—making a good impression
—crying and expressing your feelings
—making good money

The Bible sees it differently. You can earn the respect of women and others by treating them correctly. That means

—don't be selfish
—don't live to make a good impression
—be humble
—be interested in what others are doing
—have the attitude Christ had of serving others

You'll notice the difference in the two lists; one builds up you and your accomplishments; the second one (drawn from the Bible) builds up other people.

You can earn respect in life from those around you as you work to put them first.

### Philippians 2:3-7

Do nothing out of selfish ambition or vain conceit, but in humility consider others better than yourselves. Each of you should look not only to your own interests, but also to the interests of others. Your attitude should be the same as that of Christ Jesus: Who, being in very nature God, did not consider equality with God something to be grasped, but made himself nothing, taking the very nature of a servant, being made in human likeness.

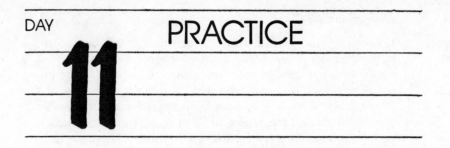

If you're involved in a sport, you know what it's like to come home in the dark, hungry and oftentimes dragging your buns. You know that practice, and lots of it, is the only way to put points on the board. Without discipline, competing seriously in a sport is little more than a joke.

The same is true of the Christian life. God doesn't ask us to be disciplined people as a way of imposing useless rules on us. He knows that without some discipline we can never grow or refine our minds and our bodies.

**Take a moment to read 1 Corinthians 9.** Paul discusses self-discipline in this chapter. Without self-control and discipline, he implies, we can't live with confidence.

Are you struggling in your Christian walk? The first thing to check on is how regularly you read God's Word and talk to Him. You really can't expect to be close to Him just by going to church on Sunday. Remember that Christianity is not just a religion, and it's more than a set of rules. It's a relationship with the God of the universe who cares about you. He wants to spend time with you alone, so you can get to know Him better, much as you spend time getting to know a friend. But unless you discipline yourself to take that time regularly, you're hardly even in the race, let alone near the front of the line.

### 1 Corinthians 9:24–27

Do you not know that in a race all the runners run, but only one gets the prize? Run in such a way as to get the prize. Everyone who competes in the games goes into strict training.

They do it to get a crown that will not last; but we do it to get a crown that will last forever. Therefore I do not run like a man running aimlessly; I do not fight like a man beating the air. No, I beat my body and make it my slave so that after I have preached to others, I myself will not be disqualified for the prize.

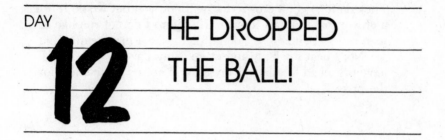

# 12

# HE DROPPED THE BALL!

Do you ever feel like you're not worth much? In an honest moment, many guys would admit they wished they were smarter, taller, built better, or came from a different home. Our world is so into visual and temporary impressions that we sometimes wonder what we are really worth when we don't measure up.

Do you know your value as a person goes way beyond what you might feel you're worth? **Take some time to read what the Bible has to say about worth in 1 John 4:9–17.** When we don't believe in ourselves (lack of self-esteem), we carry some unnecessary baggage through life. Poor self-esteem makes you act cocky; it makes you overly fearful to give a speech, to ask a girl out. You drop footballs, fail tests, and hurt other people by your actions sometimes.

Believing in your value is important to growing up. And for you to believe in yourself, you'll need to understand what is really true, not what TV and the movies might imply.

The verses in 1 John say something important about your value. Your worth is measured by what God was willing to do to keep you out of hell and to provide you with a better life while you're on earth. When the Almighty God of the universe does something for *you*, it's worth taking note of. In addition, He has given you talent and ability to do certain things well. And if you took time to notice, you'd see He's blessed you in other ways, too. One more thing to remember is that sin has a way of eroding your sense of worth. The more sin in your life, the easier it is *not* to believe in yourself.

As a Christian, God has drawn you out of a great crowd of

people. Why? Because He saw in you a worthwhile person whom He loved and could use. This makes you very valuable.

Take a minute to consider this—*you* may not be happy with how you feel, how you look, or where you came from, but these things don't matter to God. Nor does He care how bad you are. You are loved by God, forgiven by God, kept by God, and encouraged to do good by the same God who holds the universe together. And *that* makes *you* worth something.

### 1 John 4:9–12

This is how God showed his love among us: He sent his one and only Son into the world that we might live through him. This is love: not that we loved God, but that he loved us and sent his Son as an atoning sacrifice for our sins. Dear friends, since God so loved us, we also ought to love one another. No one has ever seen God; but if we love each other, God lives in us and his love is made complete in us.

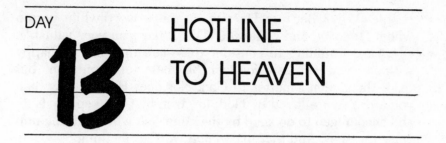

# HOTLINE
# TO HEAVEN

*Dear Lord, if it's Your will that I ask Karen out, then let me see her walking alone after fourth-period study hall.*

Did you ever pray a prayer like that? Lots of people have. That seems like a regular enough prayer, until Karen comes walking down the hall alone after third-period chemistry—a whole hour early. Your throat goes dry, and your heartbeat doubles. You can hardly believe that God would do that. What does He want anyway?

Obviously the question of whether God answers prayers is a lot more serious than what you just read about. But many people have some strange ideas about prayer and how or if God answers.

**If you'd like some new insight into this whole matter of prayer, read Romans 8:24–39.** Praying is vital to your Christian growth. Because God looks at us as His friends, prayer becomes the way you and God communicate as friends. But let's get real for a moment. How can we talk to the God of the universe? Is it possible that He would take an interest in us? The Bible says yes. And it says here in Romans that when we pray, God's spirit helps bridge the communication gap between God and us. So when you pray, God hears your prayer correctly.

What is the bottom line? God promised to hear us when we pray, but He did not promise to answer our prayers according to our wishes. This doesn't seem fair or right does it? The thing you have to remember is that God knows better than you do what is best for you, both in the short run (dates with Karen) and the long run (who you should marry).

Although it may be difficult sometimes, you'll be much

better off in life if you take everything to God and then accept the results. Remember whether God says yes, no, or wait awhile to your prayer, you can be sure that God has your very best interests at heart.

### Romans 8:26–28

In the same way, the Spirit helps us in our weakness. We do not know what we ought to pray, but the Spirit himself intercedes for us with groans that words cannot express. And he who searches our hearts knows the mind of the Spirit, because the Spirit intercedes for the saints in accordance with God's will. And we know that in all things God works for the good of those who love him, who have been called according to his purpose.

**"God knows better than you do what is best for you, both in the short run and the long run."**

# DON'T TRIP!

Cross-country running is an endurance sport. In some ways it trains an athlete better than many sports. When a runner is in a tight race he will win or lose based on *his* abilities and training, not those of the guy running next to him. His team can support him with cheers, but the race will be determined by him alone.

Life is a lot like that. We have family, friends, or a church to support us, but the big decisions rest with us.

**Take some time to read Hebrews 12:1-13.** Any cross-country runner will tell you that learning to deal with pain is a major challenge in his sport. There is mental pain which in a sense is false pain—it tells your mind that your body can't take three miles at this pace. That mental pain is an important obstacle to overcome.

So it is in life, too. When we are tempted, our minds argue that we *have to have* something or someone. Fulfilling our sexual urges, having a night out with the guys to party, or driving too fast for road conditions are ways in which our minds are asking for something that may not do us any good. How well you endure the pain of the moment will tell you whether you will win over the temptation.

The Bible says that at that moment we should think about Jesus and the fact that He endured temptation so we could have a model to go by. By fixing our eyes on Christ (asking Him for help), we have an inner strength to draw on.

Giving up a sexual thrill, a night of partying, a fit of anger, or a small lie will cause temporary pain. That pain comes with the territory of being a Christian. But the more you involve God in your life's race, the easier those miles will become.

### Hebrews 12:7–11

Endure hardship as discipline; God is treating you as sons. For what son is not disciplined by his father? If you are not disciplined (and everyone undergoes discipline), then you are illegitimate children and not true sons. Moreover, we have all had human fathers who disciplined us and we respected them for it. How much more should we submit to the Father of our spirits and live! Our fathers disciplined us for a little while as they thought best, but God disciplines us for our good, that we may share in his holiness. No discipline seems pleasant at the time, but painful. Later on, however, it produces a harvest of righteousness and peace for those who have been trained by it.

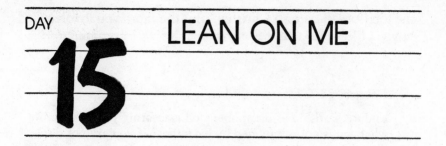

# LEAN ON ME

Have you ever had someone tell you you needed to have faith that God would take care of something? Maybe you were hurting from breaking up with your girl friend or you needed one hundred more bucks to buy a car. It's easy for someone else to say you need faith, but what does it really mean when you're in a tough situation?

It doesn't take faith to sit down in a chair—you can see very well that the chair will hold you and you'll be safe. Real faith is shown when you don't know what the results will be. When you follow God even when you can't imagine things could work out—that's faith.

**Take a moment to read Hebrews 11 and see how some people displayed their faith in God despite incredible obstacles.**

Isn't it amazing how much faith Noah, Abraham, Sarah, and the others mentioned in this chapter had in God? They trusted Him even when what they were told to do seemed ridiculous—even at the risk of being laughed at and ridiculed by their friends and relatives.

Some people were beaten to death, but they remained faithful to the God they believed in. They believed that God had something better for them, even when they didn't understand everything that happened to them.

This kind of faith isn't easy, and it doesn't come cheap. You may not be asked to suffer physically for knowing Christ personally, but you will have many opportunities to display faith in Him, even when it doesn't seem to make complete sense. Marrying the right girl, choosing a college, moving to a new town—in all these decisions and many more you will need to have faith. What it really boils down to is believing that God knows better than you what is best for you. Do you believe that?

### Hebrews 11:6-10

And without faith it is impossible to please God, because anyone who comes to him must believe that he exists and that he rewards those who earnestly seek him.

By faith Noah, when warned about things not yet seen, in holy fear built an ark to save his family. By his faith he condemned the world and became heir of the righteousness that comes by faith.

By faith Abraham, when called to go to a place he would later receive as his inheritance, obeyed and went, even though he did not know where he was going. By faith he made his home in the promised land like a stranger in a foreign country; he lived in tents, as did Isaac and Jacob, who were heirs with him of the same promise. For he was looking forward to the city with foundations, whose architect and builder is God.

# 16

# A ONE-WAY
# TICKET TO . . .

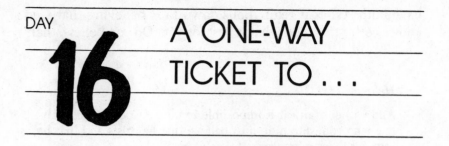

As great as it is to live in North America, there is one force at work that can be dangerous to Christians. The force? Popular thought. Popular thought is really the spoken (and unspoken) messages that are presented in advertising, entertainment, locker rooms, classes, and so on. The messages emphasize

—beauty (Feelin' Black Velvet)
—sensual enjoyment ("Let's Get Physical")
—pride in achievement or material gain
("Nobody Does It Better")

When in their proper places there is nothing wrong with beauty, sensuality, or pride in achievement. Out of place, they're devastating to a Christian.

**First John 2:15–17 has some good thoughts on this. Take a minute to read it.** On the surface, these verses sound as if they're saying Christians shouldn't enjoy life in this world, and if they do, God is not part of their lives. If you get hung up there, you'll miss the real meaning. The writer of these verses seems to have had energetic, fun-loving, and "with it" Christians in mind here. These verses are not a one-way ticket to boredom and a restricted life-style. Rather they are strong warnings to stay *balanced*. And to be aware of the *popular thought* in your culture.

We live in a society that is obsessed with physical beauty, sex, and material possessions. Sadly, all of these good things which God has given to man have been distorted and used wrongly. And the pressure is really on you today to think and behave like people who don't know God. The Lord wants to preserve you from the tragedy of endless pursuit of what popular thought says is important.

Today, God can help you

—appreciate beauty instead of lust
—keep sex in proper balance in your life
—realize all achievements and material goods are blessings from Him

### 1 John 2:15–17

Do not love the world or anything in the world. If anyone loves the world, the love of the Father is not in him. For everything in the world—the cravings of sinful man, the lust of his eyes and the boasting of what he has and does—comes not from the Father but from the world. The world and its desires pass away, but the man who does the will of God lives forever.

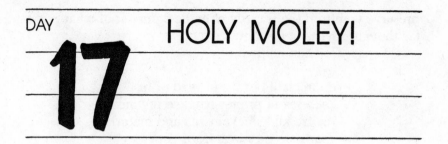

# HOLY MOLEY!

*Holiness.* The very word strikes terror in the hearts of most of us who really enjoy life. Somehow we feel that doing things God's way (that's one definition of *holiness*) and our desire to enjoy life just don't mix. Is being holy something just for your grandmother or the preacher? If you're holy, does that mean that you won't be able to T.P. the coach's house or have a car rally or kiss your girl friend? **To get some insights into this whole idea of holiness, take a minute and read 1 Peter 1:13-25.**

You probably noticed that this is one of those spots in the Bible where the writer seemed to say something not only very confusing ("Be holy, because I am holy"), but also very difficult to do. How can you *be* holy like God when you can't see Him or talk to Him face-to-face? Well, one of the great things about the Bible is that it rarely says something confusing without also providing a solution nearby.

Several of the keys for being holy are found in the first part of what you just read in 1 Peter. You noticed it gave three things to do:

1. *Prepare your minds for actions.* That means *think.* Use your head and avoid *in advance* those situations where you might be tempted to do wrong.
2. *Be self-controlled.* This is a tough one for everyone, but it means quit kissing your girl friend *before* it gets too heavy. It means go light on the gas pedal in the car when you're on the open road.
3. *Don't conform to evil desires.* Dig in and fight those atti-

tudes or thoughts that you know hurt you and your walk with God.

You can breathe easy. God is not out to make your life a drag. Rather, He wants a good and exciting life for you. The guidelines He gives us about holiness in 1 Peter are His way of helping us have the very best life has to offer.

### 1 Peter 1:13–16

Therefore, prepare your minds for action; be self-controlled; set your hope fully on the grace to be given you when Jesus Christ is revealed. As obedient children, do not conform to the evil desires you had when you lived in ignorance. But just as he who called you is holy, so be holy in all you do, for it is written: "Be holy, because I am holy."

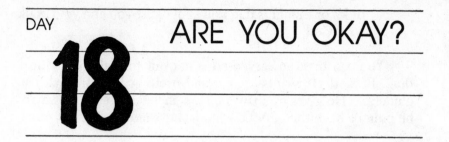

DAY **18** ARE YOU OKAY?

Yesterday we talked about holiness and how God is rather insistent about us making a real effort to be holy like Him. God wants us to be holy, not to make life a drag, but rather to help insure that we get the very best that life has to offer. Today, let's look at what happens when we decide to buck the system God has set up and do things our way. **Take a minute and read James 1:1-18.**

Did you notice the pattern described in verses 14 and 15?

1. Our evil desires tempt us. ("I'd sure like to go drinking just once.")
2. If we give in to these desires, then we sin. (Two sixpacks later, you're plastered.)
3. Too much sin leads to death. (If you do make it home safely, you feel like you let yourself, your parents, and God down.)

Have you ever noticed how sin has a weird way of making you feel sick inside? Oftentimes when we sin, we suffer a deep disappointment in ourselves. This sense of disappointment comes from God. It is guilt and is designed by God to warn us when there is sin in our lives. You can pick any sin—drinking, anger, pride, lust, hatred, and so on—and if you let it go long enough in your life, it will have a way of hurting you inside. The best way to describe that hurt is death.

God has a better idea. His word for it is *holiness*. Take some time today and check out your own life. What's happening inside you? Whatever you find, God wants to help you with it.

### James 1:12–15

Blessed is the man who perseveres under trial, because when he has stood the test, he will receive the crown of life that God has promised to those who love him.

When tempted, no one should say, "God is tempting me." For God cannot be tempted by evil, nor does he tempt anyone; but each one is tempted when, by his own evil desire, he is dragged away and enticed. Then, after desire has conceived, it gives birth to sin; and sin, when it is full-grown, gives birth to death.

*Psychologists say that men think about women and love 7 times per . . .*

# KEEP COOL

What does a girl really want in a guy? Sex appeal? Security? A comfortable living?

The answer to this question really would depend on the girl you talk to. Girls who know God personally, should (but don't always) think differently than those who live without God in their lives.

While we can't determine exactly what a girl wants, there is one quality you can develop which should be important to a girl.

**Take a minute and read Titus 2:1–8.**

One word stands out above the others—*self-control*. Self-control is one of the most difficult qualities to build and maintain in life. Everything in the world that is fun or feels good pulls us away from being self-controlled.

The Bible says self-control is a quality both men and women need. If this quality is needed by both, then it obviously is something important to others and ourselves. What does it look like? Here are some examples of what self-control is:

1. Living a life that is balanced in how much and what you eat, who you spend time with, how you spend your free time.
2. Reading the Bible when you don't feel like it.
3. Putting a stop to kissing your date if it gets out of hand.
4. Studying for a test when a good movie is on TV.
5. Not swearing when all the other guys are.

Self-control is a quality you'll need all your life. It will help you get along with teachers and employers. It will help you stay faithful to your wife and faithful to God too. Ask the Lord today to help you see where you lack self-control. Then ask Him to make you sensitive to His guidance at those moments when you have to make a hard choice.

### Titus 2:6–8

Similarly, encourage the young men to be self-controlled. In everything set them an example by doing what is good. In your teaching show integrity, seriousness and soundness of speech that cannot be condemned, so that those who oppose you may be ashamed because they have nothing bad to say about us.

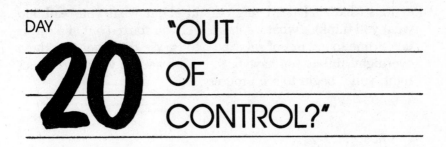

# 20 "OUT OF CONTROL?"

God never intended for your relationship with Him to be a drag. From the beginning, God's idea was to have you and others as His friends. If you listen to some Christians, it's easy to get fouled up on this and think God wants you to act more holy and be more spiritual. It's not true. God is looking to have a friend in you and be a friend in return. **Take a moment and read James 2:21–24.**

Abraham was a friend of God because of a very important fact—he *said* he would obey God and then *backed it up* with action. This same combination of believing in God and then acting right which made Abraham a friend of God can make you a friend of God's too. Two things are worth remembering:

1. Faith isn't what you might think. "Just have more faith in God and you won't struggle with masturbation anymore." These kinds of statements just aren't true. Faith is the confidence we have that something we want is going to happen. You need faith to believe in a God you can't see. Faith in God is the engine of your life. It motivates (moves) you to do right.

2. Faith isn't enough in life. You'll need to act right too. Right actions (driving the car of your life in the right direction) come from talking regularly with God (asking for directions), reading the Bible (the road map), and then just living (hitting the road).

Do you feel trapped by masturbation or something else in your life? Combining faith that God can help you and the right actions (that includes being careful about what you read and what you think) is what it takes to get you started out of a rut. It takes time to get out of ruts and habits. We don't get into them overnight. But as you have faith in God and do your part to act right, you'll begin to see progress.

### James 2:21-24

Was not our ancestor Abraham considered righteous for what he did when he offered his son Isaac on the altar? You see that his faith and his actions were working together, and his faith was made complete by what he did. And the scripture was fulfilled that says, "Abraham believed God, and it was credited to him as righteousness," and he was called God's friend. You see that a person is justified by what he does and not by faith alone.

We all assume that girls are more emotional ("She just got real emotional and started crying and everything") than guys ("big boys don't cry"). Generally speaking that's true. But that doesn't mean guys are *never* emotional or girls are *always* so emotional they can't think straight. In fact, sometimes big boys *do* cry and it's good for them. Everyone has emotions. Since you are a guy, your emotions are wired differently than a girl's to be sure. But that doesn't mean there's no room to admit you get the blues sometimes.

How do you handle feeling down? Do you hide it? Pretend it's not there? **Take a few minutes to read Psalm 139. It has some promises worth considering when you feel blue.**

The Bible says here that God knows your thoughts before you think them; He knows when you wake up and when you lie down. When you were growing inside your mother, God was forming your body *and* your emotions. Whether you feel elated or depressed, God will be with you, guiding you, and holding you in His hand.

It should encourage you that from the moment you were conceived until you die, God has complete knowledge of your life, its joys and its hurts. You will not always feel like God is in control, just like you won't always feel like you are a Christian. Strong feelings have a way of masking the truth so it becomes difficult to see what is real. Feelings change rapidly too, sometimes leaving you feeling unsettled.

But your feelings or lack of them don't change the facts. God knows you, understands you, and is actively at work on your behalf. This is a promise you can count on, no matter how you feel. In the future when you feel emotional, take a minute to ask God to help you recall what He has promised.

### Psalms 139:1–4

O Lord, you have searched me and you know me. You know when I sit and when I rise; you perceive my thoughts from afar. You discern my going out and my lying down; you are familiar with all my ways. Before a word is on my tongue you know it completely, O Lord.

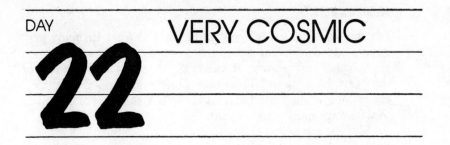

# VERY COSMIC

How smart would you figure God is? One of the words used to describe God is *omniscience*. That's one of those Christian words floating around which simply means God knows everything. Another way to look at it is that He created the recipe *and* the ingredients for pizza—all the pizzas in life.

God's incredible knowledge actually is rather important to you. **To understand more about God's wisdom, take some time to read Hebrews 4:12–16.**

Everything you have ever said or done, how far you've gone with a girl, the tests you've cheated on, the lies you told your mom and dad—all are known to God.

Most of us do not live our lives every day as if God knew all about us. We would probably live differently if we did. Someday you will have to give an explanation to God for *why* you lived the way you did. The point is, God can't stand sin in your life. And He will work gently (by convincing you through his Word and your conscience) and firmly (using an event or disappointment) to help you see your need to change an attitude or an action.

Because God is all-knowing, you can also trust Him with your life. He understands the absolute best route for you to take in life, so your life counts for something more than a string of good times.

Realizing that God is all-knowing should concern you and motivate you to live more carefully. But it should also help you breathe easier as you think about your future. There is no better place to be than to be depending on an all-knowing God for direction. Involve God in your life. You'll never regret it.

*Hebrews 4:12, 13*

For the word of God is living and active. Sharper than any double-edged sword, it penetrates even to dividing soul and spirit, joints and marrow; it judges the thoughts and attitudes of the heart. Nothing in all creation is hidden from God's sight. Everything is uncovered and laid bare before the eyes of him to whom we must give account.

**"Involve God in your life. You'll never regret it."**

# 23

# GIFTS FROM GOD

Almost everyone has had the experience of feeling inadequate in some area. There's a lot of pressure on a guy to be a leader, be active in sports, and be the best at what he does. But what if you aren't particularly athletic, or handsome, or talented in the way you'd like to be? How can you accept yourself as you are, as God made you, when you feel that everyone else is so much better at everything than you are?

**See what 1 Corinthians 12 has to say about this.**

We all have gifts and talents which can be used, no matter how small they may seem to us. This passage describes how important it is for each person (part of the body) to do its thing, so that the entire body can function well. That's why there's no reason to play the comparison game. God doesn't rate one gift any better than another. And He doesn't ask us to function in ways we aren't capable of. He just asks that we give what we have to Him to be used for His purposes. Many of us spend a lot of time and energy trying to be something we're not. When we don't accept ourselves, we make it difficult for God to show His power through us.

Can you take a few minutes to list some of the talents or gifts you consider yourself blessed with? Will you pick one of these that you particularly like and ask God to develop the quality in you for His service? But don't ask Him to do it unless you really mean it.

### *1 Corinthians 12:12, 13, 24-26*

The body is a unit, though it is made up of many parts; and though all its parts are many, they form one body. So it is with Christ. For we were all baptized by one Spirit into one body—whether Jews or Greeks, slave or free—and we were all given the one Spirit to drink. . . . But God has combined the members of the body and has given greater honor to the parts that lacked it, so that there should be no division in the body, but that its parts should have equal concern for each other. If one part suffers, every part suffers with it; if one part is honored, every part rejoices with it.

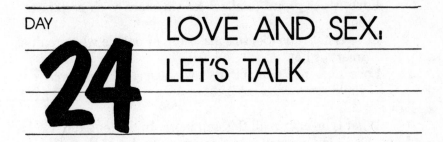

# LOVE AND SEX: LET'S TALK

By this point in your life, you know girls think differently than you do about love. Just when you want to find a nice quiet place to "talk," she gets in one of her athletic moods and wants to run two miles! Everyone seems to have a different definition of *love*. If you listen to the Top Twenty or go to the movies, you get a different view of love. If your mom or dad are divorced, you probably wonder if love is really worth looking forward to. What is love really like? A feeling? Are you in love now? How do you know if someone else loves you?

**Take a moment to read a well-known chapter in the Bible about love: 1 Corinthians 13.** Paul wrote this letter to people who lived in a wild and crazy city (Corinth) where love was almost completely expressed by sex—and bizarre sex at that.

Love is certainly a feeling, but the feelings are not the most important part of love. Love is also action and motivation.

Love is patient and kind (waits for the bathroom without grumbling).

Love is loyal (sticks up for a friend when he's not present to defend himself in a conversation).

Love believes in someone (encourages a friend to tell the truth).

Love expects the best from someone (helps his date believe in herself).

Love defends someone (says something good about his parents even though everyone else cuts theirs down).

Love is not jealous (compliments his brother on good grades).

Love is not proud (realizes he was born with certain talents).

Love is not rude (doesn't make fun of people who aren't as smart as he).

Love does not demand its own way ("If you loved me, you'd sleep with me").

What is love? It is all this and more. In the long run, God is Love. Don't kid yourself into thinking something is love when it isn't. If you are wondering how well you love or if you are in love, try measuring your feelings against what the Bible says true love is. The results might surprise you.

### 1 Corinthians 13:4–7

Love is patient, love is kind. It does not envy, it does not boast, it is not proud. It is not rude, it is not self-seeking, it is not easily angered, it keeps no record of wrongs. Love does not delight in evil but rejoices with the truth. It always protects, always trusts, always hopes, always perseveres.

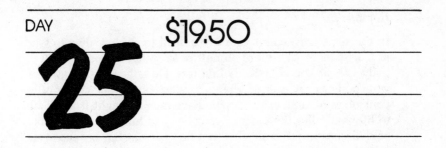
Throughout your life you will meet Christians who have different standards than you. Some may be so strict they won't associate with you. Some will say it doesn't really matter what we do or how we live since our sins will be forgiven.

**Take a moment to read Romans 6 for some insight into this discussion about sin.**

Apparently, the Christians in Rome were assuming they could live any way they wanted to and still be followers of Christ. In many ways, they were betraying Christ by allowing various sins to control them. And they were putting other things before God.

Sometimes we see sin clearly, because it's obvious. But at other times, we kind of slide into it—inch by inch—and before we know it, we've taken a big fall. Sexual sins often happen that way. It seems so innocent and right at the time. But impure behavior makes us slaves to sin. It's much more difficult to do the right thing the next time, if you've allowed yourself to go farther than you should have on your last date. That's how sin traps us and makes us slaves to it.

The story of Judas betraying Jesus is well-known to most people. Did you realize he betrayed Jesus for thirty shekels, or about $19.50? It seems so crazy, and yet, in many ways, we daily betray God by living selfishly, continuing in sinful behavior, and putting possessions or people before God. What about you? Are there sins you continue to be trapped in? Are you putting something before Christ? Talk to Him about it.

## Romans 6:11–14

In the same way, count yourselves dead to sin but alive to God in Christ Jesus. Therefore do not let sin reign in your mortal body so that you obey its evil desires. Do not offer the parts of your body to sin, as instruments of wickedness, but rather offer yourselves to God, as those who have been brought from death to life; and offer the parts of your body to him as instruments of righteousness. For sin shall not be your master, because you are not under law, but under grace.

*Ladies and gentlemen, it appears our contender is in some kind of trouble!*

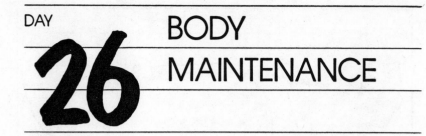

# BODY MAINTENANCE

*Physical.* What does that word mean to you? Well-built, good-looking girls? Pumping iron? Smelly locker rooms? Yelling coaches? Chowing-down pizza? Making out?

No matter what your shape or size is, whether you're eating, working out, or kissing your girl friend good night, your body shows up for the performance.

Believe it or not, God is concerned about the physical aspects of your life, and He's concerned about what you put in it, wear on it, where you take it, and who you share it with.

**For more insight into what God's Word has to say about your body read Daniel 1:8–21 and 1 Corinthians 10:31.**

The verses in Daniel clearly show that when Daniel honored the way he was taught, God blessed him with good health and position.

The verse in Corinthians helps us even more. What you put into your body and what you do with it should be done so that neither God's reputation nor yours is damaged. When it comes to your body, one word is worth remembering—*balance.*

Take a minute right now and check yourself on the following:

Where have you taken your body in the past month? (bars, Bible study, gymnasium, running track?)

What have you put in it? (junk food, vegetables, booze, smoke?)

How much of your body have you shared with someone else?

Keeping our relationship with God intact is the most important thing in life. How we handle our bodies can affect that important relationship. Handling your body carefully not only brings you self-respect, but pleases God also.

### Daniel 1:15–17

At the end of the ten days they looked healthier and better nourished than any of the young men who ate the royal food. So the guard took away their choice food and the wine they were to drink and gave them vegetables instead. To these four young men God gave knowledge and understanding of all kinds of literature and learning. And Daniel could understand visions and dreams of all kinds.

### 1 Corinthians 10:31

So whether you eat or drink or whatever you do, do it all for the glory of God.

# 27

# I FEEL ROTTEN!

Have you ever felt that you'd done something so terrible that God could never forgive you? Maybe you went a little too far on a date with your girl friend, cheated on a test, got high, or blew your witness by telling a dirty joke. Perhaps you asked God to forgive you, but inside you still felt guilty. Or maybe you just feel like you're such a nothing that God could never really care about or use you for anything important.

**Take a moment to read 1 Timothy 1:12–17.**

Consider this guy, Paul. Talk about an unlikely candidate for God's work. At one time he was directly responsible for killing Christians. He took it upon himself, before he believed in Christ, to track down Christians and have them murdered. But there is no sin too big or too terrible for God to forgive. The Old Testament is full of stories of people who sinned against God— liars, egotists, cheaters, you name it—and yet, when they asked for forgiveness and continued following Him, God forgave them and used their lives to please Himself.

This doesn't mean we should sin just to prove God can use us. But since we all do sin, we need to ask Him often to forgive us and keep us on the right track. God isn't looking for super people—He's looking for basic people who will acknowledge their sins and turn to Him. They're the only people He can use.

What about you? Do you believe God can clear the slate and use your life?

### 1 Timothy 1:15–17

Here is a trustworthy saying that deserves full acceptance: Christ Jesus came into the world to save sinners—of whom I am the worst. But for that very reason I was shown mercy so that in me, the worst of sinners, Christ Jesus might display his unlimited patience as an example for those who would believe on him and receive eternal life. Now to the King eternal, immortal, invisible, the only God, be honor and glory for ever and ever. Amen.

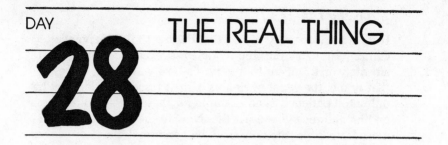

# THE REAL THING

When was the last time you pulled the tab on a can of Pepsi and said to yourself, *I wonder if they really put Pepsi in this can.*

Obviously, few of us walk around thinking like that, and the people we know who do are generally not president of Student Council or at the head of the class. We open Pepsi cans and expect Pepsi, step on gas pedals and expect the car to move, climb on school buses and expect to end up at school. In a word—we *trust.*

When you stop to think about it, there are lots of things we do in a day that require us to trust. *Trust* is one of those words some Christians throw around or use lightly. "Just trust God," sounds great but can be tough to do sometimes.

The Bible has something to say about *where* to put our confidence. **Take a minute and read Jeremiah 17:5-8.** In simple terms these verses say, *Trust in yourself* and you will *find yourself alone* when big decisions need answers. ("Where should I go to college?") And you will *find yourself without roots* when temptation hits. ("I really didn't want to go that far with her, but somehow I didn't have the strength to stop.")

In life, you will face lots of little but important decisions as well as several big ones. How well you will make those decisions is directly related to whether you trust your own common sense or God's. The Bible promises that when we put our confidence in God, we become more *stable* and *have less to worry about* when we face tough decisions.

Do you *trust* God by asking Him to help you make good

decisions? You know, God's got common sense. By simply asking Him to help you with your decisions, you can have confidence that God will lead you right.

### Jeremiah 17:5-8

This is what the Lord says: "Cursed is the one who trusts in man, who depends on flesh for his strength and whose heart turns away from the Lord. He will be like a bush in the wastelands; he will not see prosperity when it comes. He will dwell in the parched places of the desert, in a salt land where no one lives. But blessed is the man who trusts in the Lord, whose confidence is in him. He will be like a tree planted by the water that sends out its roots by the stream. It does not fear when heat comes; its leaves are always green. It has no worries in a year of drought and never fails to bear fruit."

# BECAUSE I SAID SO!

Now let's be very honest for a moment. Parents can say some pretty strange things. "Make your bed, company is coming." (Company never goes in your bedroom.) "What time are you coming home?" (Oh brother! How can they ask that when they threaten to skin you alive if you're one minute past curfew?) But the classic of all time is the one statement that is music to your parents' ears and downright painful to yours— "BECAUSE I SAID SO!" Why do parents say that? It's anybody's guess.

It can really make you mad when parents say, "Because I said so." And do you know what? Parents are wrong for saying it. But if you handle it wrong, get mad or bitter, then things can get real tough. The Bible has something to say about how we handle our anger. **Take a minute to read Ephesians 4:23-32.**

These verses talk about personal growth. They put an emphasis on attitudes changing, truthfulness, and handling our anger carefully. Actually, these verses are as much for young people as they are for adults. That means when your parents say, "Because I said so," and you get ticked, you have a responsibility to go to them and tell them your feelings and work out the differences. This kind of openness can help the communication process tremendously. Ask God to help you be honest with your parents and to give you the right attitude about talking to them. As you work on your attitude and go to bed mad less often, you'll find that accepting some of the strange things your parents say will get easier. With God's help you can have a good influence on your parents and do your part to make home a better place to live.

*Ephesians 4:29-32*

Do not let any unwholesome talk come out of your mouths, but only what is helpful for building others up according to their needs, that it may benefit those who listen. And do not grieve the Holy Spirit of God, with whom you were sealed for the day of redemption. Get rid of all bitterness, rage and anger, brawling and slander, along with every form of malice. Be kind and compassionate to one another, forgiving each other, just as in Christ God forgave you.

# HANG LOOSE

## 30

You will be pleased to know that getting restless as a Christian is not a new phenomenon nor a sign that you're not a Christian anymore. Since the time of Jesus, sincere Christians (even preachers and saints) felt the pressure to wander away from their faith. **For some insight into this read John 20:19-31.**

Thomas was not any different from most of us. We want hard, tangible proof that being a Christian is worth it. Jesus said to Thomas, "Don't be faithless any longer. Believe." Actually, believing in Jesus today is much harder than it was for Thomas. Computers and television have made us skeptical of the supernatural—of things we can't see and figure out. Not being able to figure something out leads to doubting, and doubting leads to restlessness.

In the 1700s a restless Christian by the name of Robert Robinson wrote a verse to a hymn which is still sung today— "Come Thou Fount of Every Blessing." It'll sound like Shakespeare a little, but read it through.

> Prone to wander, Lord I feel it,
> Prone to leave the God I love;
> Here's my heart, O take and seal it
> Seal it for thy courts above.

Restlessness is a part of our culture. It will always be there as a force, pulling us away from important things, such as school and church and family. Like rebellion, restlessness can only hurt you if you don't channel it into something constructive like a prayer to the Lord. If you get restless with being a Christian, take some time to talk to God. Open up and tell Him what you feel. Remember it's His religion and He wants to help you with your feelings about it.


### John 20:24-29

Now Thomas (called Didymus), one of the Twelve, was not with the disciples when Jesus came. When the other disciples told him that they had seen the Lord, he declared, "Unless I see the nail marks in his hands and put my finger where the nails were, and put my hand into his side, I will not believe it." A week later his disciples were in the house again, and Thomas was with them. Though the doors were locked, Jesus came and stood among them and said, "Peace be with you!" Then he said to Thomas, "Put your finger here; see my hands. Reach out your hand and put it into my side. Stop doubting and believe." Thomas said to him, "My Lord and my God!" Then Jesus told him, "Because you have seen me, you have believed; blessed are those who have not seen and yet have believed."

*Goin' places—I wonder if God knows where I'm going?*

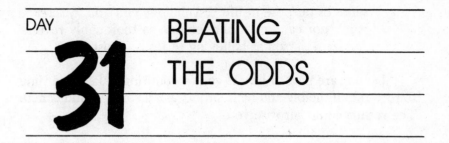

# BEATING
# THE ODDS

If there were some way to prove that Christianity is not real or God isn't going to deliver on the heaven thing, you can bet there would be a lot of people who would live differently.

Do you ever wonder whether Christianity is worth it? If there really is a God who answers prayer? Doubts are part of the process of believing in God and taking Him at His word. The Bible has some encouraging words about whether we can rationally believe in God. **Take a minute and read Psalms 8:3, 4 and Hebrews 1:1–3.**

When you doubt, there are three things to think about:

1. It is extremely difficult to believe that all of the universe and especially the consistent order of things on Earth came about without the intervention of a supreme intelligence. Just the abilities of man's brain and his hands have never been successfully produced by man. Even to scientists, humans seem to be a copy (image) of something not found on Earth.

2. The Book we call the Bible is unique. No religious book has ever withstood the criticism this Book has and still remained a best-seller. It defies the odds. And it also states it is the official writing and history of the supreme intelligent Being who claims to have created the heavens and Earth.

3. Believing and practicing what is in this Book changes people's lives. Somehow putting faith in the God/Man Jesus Christ written about in the Book changes murderers and liars; it frees people from guilt; it gives people a

sense of purpose in life. Psychology can't do it, science can't, nor can any other religion so thoroughly revolutionize a person as believing in Jesus Christ.

Doubts are part of life. If you're doubting, take some time to recount all the big and little proofs you have that God is real. The results could surprise you.

### Psalms 8:3,4

When I consider your heavens, the work of your fingers, the moon and the stars, which you have set in place, what is man that you are mindful of him, the son of man that you care for him?

### Hebrews 1:1–3

In the past God spoke to our forefathers through the prophets at many times and in various ways, but in these last days he has spoken to us by his Son, whom he appointed heir of all things, and through whom he made the universe. The Son is the radiance of God's glory and the exact representation of his being, sustaining all things by his powerful word. After he had provided purification for sins, he sat down at the right hand of the Majesty in heaven.

# YOUR REPUTATION

# 32

"He's got a reputation for standing girls up." "She's got a reputation with guys." You can make it in life without a lot of things, but one ingredient you will need wherever you go is a good reputation. How's yours?

**Take a minute to read Proverbs 22 about reputation.**

The Bible says here that you may be faced with the choice between riches and a good name. It's interesting that this verse sets up a choice between money and a good name. If a person's reputation is tarnished, it is most often because he or she didn't handle money correctly. But you may also have to choose a good reputation over a good time (sexually) or popularity (lying to cover for a friend).

These verses also make it clear that a good name is worth more than money, a good time, or popularity. Sometimes Christians have used reputation as a club to whip people into line. "If you mess around on a date, you'll get a reputation." "If you don't tell the truth, you'll get a reputation."

While it is true that people know us by how we act, the real reason for living correctly should be to please God, not because we fear what others will say.

One final thing to remember. You can always rebuild a tarnished reputation. God forgives and forgets your past mistakes. He wants to be involved in helping you live right so you can rebuild or maintain a good name in the future.

### Proverbs 22:1-6

A good name is more desirable than great riches; to be esteemed is better than silver or gold. Rich and poor have this in common: The Lord is the Maker of them all. A prudent man sees danger and takes refuge, but the simple keep going and suffer for it. Humility and the fear of the Lord bring wealth and honor and life. In the paths of the wicked lie thorns and snares, but he who guards his soul stays far from them. Train a child in the way he should go, and when he is old he will not turn from it.

# GOD'S XEROX

When Jesus Christ came into your life, He changed you, turned your life around, and gave you hope and peace. This process was no accident. God was in it the whole way, and He used other people to get the job done in your life.

God's Word has something to say to you about the importance of duplicating this process in the lives of your friends and relatives. Like the cure for cancer, being a Christian is so valuable that we should share it with others.

**Take some time to read Romans 10:1–15.**

Generally, there are two types of Christians: those who want to be *silent witnesses* and those who are leaving tracts in the washroom and holding evangelistic services at the bus stop. Neither extreme is appropriate all the time. So what ends up happening is that the *silent witness* people rarely, if ever, make a verbal attempt to share their new lives in Christ with others, and the *fanatics* go around turning people off by their approach. Is there a middle ground? You bet.

Today, God needs people who know Him and who can be mature enough to say in public what they believe in private. Fear of being rejected or losing popularity is the number-one reason most Christian high school students can't share their faith in Christ with others.

So they remain silent witnesses while their friends have abortions, get drunk, and break the law. Here are some simple ideas on how to tell others about God:

1. You don't necessarily have to pray before every lunch, but a regular quiet prayer lets your friends know God is in your life.
2. You can invite some friends to a Bible study. But be sure you have open discussion about what you read. Don't hold a church service.
3. If you've got a good youth group in your church, invite your friends to an activity.
4. Ask your friends some questions about their beliefs in God. God can open up discussion among you and give you an opportunity to share your faith.

The bottom line is that God doesn't need Christians who are going around whacking people on the head with the Bible. He *does* need together, fun-loving Christians who are willing to quit sitting on their hands and do something active to tell their friends and relatives about new life in Christ. God is ready to help you and give you courage.

### Romans 10:10–15

For it is with your heart that you believe and are justified, and it is with your mouth that you confess and are saved. As the Scripture says, "Everyone who trusts in him will never be put to shame." For there is no difference between Jew and Gentile—the same Lord is Lord of all and richly blesses all who call on him, for, "Everyone who calls on the name of the Lord will be saved." How, then, can they call on the one they have not believed in? And how can they believe in the one of whom they have not heard? And how can they hear without someone preaching to them? And how can they preach unless they are sent? As it is written, "How beautiful are the feet of those who bring good news!"

# BUZZ WORDS

Which of the following words do you recognize? *Far-out, wimp, cosmic, doobie, cool, jazzed-up, veggie, val girl, preppie, jerk, super neat?* At some point in time all these were "in" words in high schools across America.

If you've been attending church for a while you probably have noticed that there are certain "in" words (religious talk) used by Christian people.

Heard these buzz words lately? *Born again, filled with the Holy Spirit, be ye sanctified, you are justified by faith?* Oftentimes these words or phrases can lose their meaning and become boring to you. It's not uncommon for people then, to tune out some of this religious talk. When we begin to tune out other people, especially Christians who are older than us, we set ourselves up for trouble, because we cut ourselves off from their valuable input.

Yet the way some Christians talk can be a real pain. What's the solution? **Take a minute and read 2 Timothy 2:14.** You can trust the Bible to say it straight. It seems there will always be "religious" people who are into "God talk." There is no sense to quarrel with them inwardly (getting bad feelings toward the church or people) or outwardly (arguing or tuning people out). You won't change them, but you can do something constructive. The Bible says to do two things: Do your best to be presentable (win your battles with sin) before God and be a person who knows how to handle God's Word (be clear and relevant in how you talk about God and religious things to other people).

You'll never get away from religious buzz words or the Christians who use them. How you handle them will be a test of your ability to accept others and to apply what you know about being a better person.

### 2 Timothy 2:14

Keep reminding them of these things. Warn them before God against quarreling about words; it is of no value, and only ruins those who listen.

**"You can trust the Bible to say it straight."**

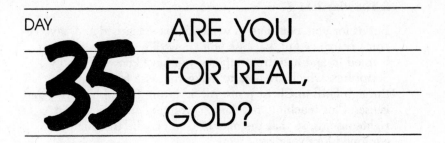

# 35 ARE YOU FOR REAL, GOD?

Can the Bible be trusted? When you think about it, Christians make some pretty big claims about the Bible. Not only do Christians say the writers of the Bible were inspired (in their thinking) to write exactly what God wanted them to say, but they also say that we can trust God's Word to have no errors in its presentation of Christ and what He did.

Can you really trust a Book that is almost two thousand years old to be true and of any value to you in your life? **Take some time and read 2 Timothy 3:14–17 three times out loud.** One verse in this passage says, "All Scripture is God-breathed." What proof do we have that the Bible came from some powerful God no one has ever seen? Here's something to think about. Forty men, in thirty different occupations, wrote the Bible in three different languages over the course of sixteen hundred years. In all, 807,367 words in the Bible work together in harmony to talk of one God, one devil, one heaven, one hell, and one way of salvation. The Bible has withstood wars, human criticism, and time to become the best selling book of all time.

But perhaps more than all of this, the best proof we have that God's Word is trustworthy is the fact that reading it, applying it, and believing it can change our lives. Because what is in the Bible are God's thoughts and insights on how to make it on Earth, it links us with a loving God. Many religions on Earth have a "holy book," but no religion has a book like the Bible, which when believed and applied can be of such hope and help to man. History proves that when man takes God's Word seriously, it works. Hey, how about your Bible? Is it working for you?

### 2 Timothy 3:14–17

But as for you, continue in what you have learned and have become convinced of, because you know those from whom you learned it, and how from infancy you have known the holy Scriptures, which are able to make you wise for salvation through faith in Christ Jesus. All Scripture is God-breathed and is useful for teaching, rebuking, correcting and training in righteousness, so that the man of God may be thoroughly equipped for every good work.

# 36

# TEN LOUSY MINUTES!

It's Friday night in October. There's a football game going on at school. You're sitting home, still stunned by the fact that your parents grounded you for coming in ten minutes late last Saturday night. Adults can be so unreasonable sometimes. What's the big deal about ten lousy minutes?

Handling adults or parents is no small task when you're a teenager. Parents seem to have such out-of-date attitudes; they get hung up over little things like ten minutes or a messy room, and the rules they want you to live by went out with hula hoops.

What's the best way to handle your parents or any adult for that matter? The Bible has some good advice. **Take some time and read Ephesians 6:1-4.** This is a good passage to sit down and talk about with your mom or dad. There's something in it for both your folks and you. You'll notice that the Bible says that fathers should not exasperate their children. Maybe if you're feeling exasperated you need to take the initiative and talk to your folks. Often teenagers have trouble with adults because of poor communication, not differences of opinion.

The important thing to remember is that God asks you to honor and respect your folks, even when you disagree with them. Believe it or not, your folks have almost twice as much experience at living as you do. They've seen their own mistakes and hurts and they want to help you avoid them. Don't let a disagreement over a movie, curfew, choice of friends, or whatever stand between you and your folks. Next time you have a hassle with your parents, whether you have one parent or two, remember this—God wants you to honor and obey them, not because "that's just the way it is," but because God has your best interest in mind and has provided adult guidance so that "it may go well with you."

### Ephesians 6:1-4

Children, obey your parents in the Lord, for this is right. "Honor your father and mother"—which is the first commandment with a promise—"that it may go well with you and that you may enjoy long life on the earth."

Fathers, do not exasperate your children; instead, bring them up in the training and instruction of the Lord.

*I wonder how loud I have to talk for God to hear me?*

# 37

# ARE YOU THERE?

When you hear the words *Holy Spirit,* what comes to mind? Our modern culture with its emphasis on logical thought, practicality, and electronic technology leaves little room for a supernatural being like the Holy Spirit. The emphasis in today's world is to distrust or doubt anything supernatural. There just doesn't seem to be any room for belief in an unseen God. Yet the Bible has something entirely different to say about God and the Holy Spirit. **Read John 14:15–21 and 25–27.**

Many young people get uncomfortable when there's any discussion about the Holy Spirit. For some reason, it just seems too far-out to deal with. And the church doesn't help much. One of the greatest disservices the church does to God is depicting the Holy Spirit as a mystical Holy Ghost who is only for super-spiritual people to have any experience with. Nothing is more untrue.

God knew that man flounders when he cannot see God. So out of love for us, the Lord provided a *comforter,* a *counselor inside us* to guide us in living.

In many ways the Holy Spirit is in our conscience, warning us of attitudes or actions that will hurt us or comforting us when we hurt. It is a mystery *how* God works in people who know Him personally. The Bible says the world can't accept this mystery. This is a danger for Christians too, who can be influenced by the world's thinking to believe the Holy Spirit isn't in them or is unimportant.

If you have asked God to forgive you of your sins and you are walking with Him, God's Spirit is in you. Today ask God to help you not to freak out over this mystery of God's presence in your life. Remember it is the world's influence that is working on you to discredit the Holy Spirit.

### John 14:15–17; 25–27

"If you love me, you will obey what I command. And I will ask the Father, and he will give you another Counselor to be with you forever—the Spirit of truth. The world cannot accept him, because it neither sees him nor knows him. But you know him, for he lives with you and will be in you. . . ." "All this I have spoken while still with you. But the Counselor, the Holy Spirit, whom the Father will send in my name, will teach you all things and will remind you of everything I have said to you. Peace I leave with you; my peace I give you. I do not give to you as the world gives. Do not let your hearts be troubled and do not be afraid."

You know that sickening feeling you have in the pit of your stomach when you know you've done something wrong? The longer you think about it, the worse it feels. Think back to the last time you did something you knew your parents wouldn't like. You probably found yourself trying to avoid them. And the longer you avoided them, the longer that gnawing feeling in your stomach continued.

It would be really dumb to say that doing what you know is wrong doesn't feel good—or that it isn't fun. But if you have truly accepted Christ into your heart, God's Spirit within you is hurt. It's as if He's been watching all along, and since He's an integral part of you, you feel uneasy over your sin.

**Take a moment to read Psalm 32.** This Psalm of David brings home what happens when we delay talking with God about sin. David pours out his thoughts in verses 3 and 4–his unconfessed sin had consequences. Once he admitted this, he knew God had forgiven him and he could once again have a good relationship with God. When you've hurt someone by something you've said or done, don't you both feel an awkwardness that continues to get worse the longer you both ignore it? The same is true in your relationship with God. If you keep ignoring what you know is separating you from Him, it will only strain the relationship and make you feel distant from God. If you feel distant from God, He is not the one who is responsible. Try talking to Him about it, much as you'd talk to a close friend. He wants to share your sorrow and your fear. If you continue to separate yourself from Him through unconfessed sin, you're hurting yourself and you're also hurting God.

Won't you take a few moments now to reflect on your relationship with God? Is everything straight between you two, or are you hiding—or trying to hide—certain things?

### Psalms 32:1-5

Blessed is he whose transgressions are forgiven, whose sins are covered. Blessed is the man whose sin the Lord does not count against him and in whose spirit is no deceit. When I kept silent, my bones wasted away through my groaning all day long. For day and night your hand was heavy upon me; my strength was sapped as in the heat of summer. Then I acknowledged my sin to you and did not cover up my iniquity. I said, "I will confess my transgressions to the Lord"—and you forgave the guilt of my sin.

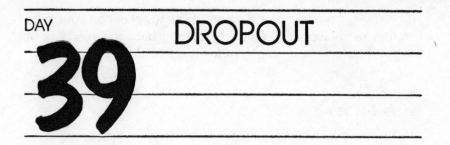

# DROPOUT

Have you ever met someone who's dropped out of the church scene because he thought there were too many hypocrites involved? Or perhaps you've witnessed people who profess to be Christians behaving in ways that go against the teachings of Christ. *If that's what a Christian is,* you may have thought, *forget it.*

**Take a moment to read 1 Corinthians 2.** Back when these words were written, some people in the church were rallying behind personalities—Christian superstars—and forgetting that the Christian faith rests on belief in God, not people. There have always been, and will always be, people in the church who claim to be Christians but don't live the life they profess. Sometimes they're even Christian leaders, like the religious leaders in Christ's time, the Pharisees.

None of us is perfect, we're all hypocrites in a way. We don't have to be perfect to be accepted by God; in fact, what we need to do is admit our imperfections.

Keeping your eyes on people is one of the quickest ways there is to burn out on Christianity. But somehow it doesn't make much sense to someday stand before God and whine, "But God, there were so many hypocrites in the church!" He'd probably agree wholeheartedly and then ask the piercing question: "But what about you? I never asked you to put your faith in people, but in Me."

What about you? Are you allowing other people to distance you from God? Are you confusing the wisdom of men with the power of God?

### 1 Corinthians 2:6–10

We do, however, speak a message of wisdom among the mature, but not the wisdom of this age or of the rulers of this age, who are coming to nothing. No, we speak of God's secret wisdom, a wisdom that has been hidden and that God destined for our glory before time began. None of the rulers of this age understood it, for if they had, they would not have crucified the Lord of glory. However, as it is written:

> "No eye has seen,
>    no ear has heard,
>  no mind has conceived
>    what God has prepared for those
>    who love him"

but God has revealed it to us by his Spirit.

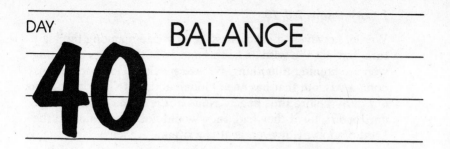

# BALANCE

Balance is one of the most important conditions man needs to maintain in life. Without balance, gymnasts break their routines, wars start, people get the flu, fires break out, banks get robbed. Throughout every area of life, balance is needed to insure quality, peace, and good health.

Balance is not often talked about among Christians. Yet the Bible is one long record of God working to bring balance into the lives of men.

Buried in the New Testament is a phenomenal little Scripture verse on balance, which is often overlooked. **Take a minute and read Luke 2:52 a couple of times.** You'll notice this verse broke the life of Jesus into four parts:

He grew in

> —wisdom (mentally)
> —stature (physically)
> —favor with God (spiritually)
> —favor with man (socially)

This little verse depicts Jesus as a person who was growing in normal ways. And because Jesus is a model for our lives, the verse becomes an important measuring stick for our personal growth. Your growing spiritually, physically, mentally, and socially is important to God. Over the next several devotions we'll look at the importance of balance in each of these areas. Remember that God is committed to balance in your life just as He was in Jesus'.

More than making you obey rules, God wants to help you

maintain balance in your life. This love of God for us is important to remember as we look at different areas of our lives.

### Luke 2:52

And Jesus grew in wisdom and stature, and in favor with God and men.

**66**... God wants to help you maintain balance in your life.**99**

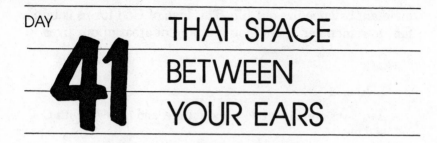

# THAT SPACE BETWEEN YOUR EARS

Most people treat their minds like they treat the school principal—unless it gives you trouble, leave it alone. Did you know that how you treat your mind matters a lot to God? He's concerned not only with what you put in it but also how you use it.

**Take some time to read Philippians 4:4-9.** If you could read this in the language the New Testament was written in—Greek—you would see the verses you just read encourage you to not only think good thoughts, but to let those thoughts shape your *attitudes* as well. That's because *what* we think has a big impact on *how* we act.

Thinking correctly is a vital part of being a balanced person. The verse you read yesterday (Luke 2:52) said Jesus grew in wisdom as well as physically. Jesus could never have done what He did unless He developed and used His mind correctly.

Do you want to be a smart person? Maybe you're getting good grades already and you can hold your own in most any conversation with an adult; but the Bible says that is not true wisdom. The Bible says respect for God is the beginning of wisdom. And this respect isn't related to how smart you are. It's something anyone can do.

In Philippians we get practical guidance on what to think about. This kind of thinking can keep you balanced so that your mind doesn't become a garbage can for the latest thing the world might be pushing. Remember—garbage in, garbage out. Your mind is worth more. Both to God and to you.

## Philippians 4:4-9

Rejoice in the Lord always. I will say it again: Rejoice! Let your gentleness be evident to all. The Lord is near. Do not be anxious about anything, but in everything, by prayer and petition, with thanksgiving, present your requests to God. And the peace of God, which transcends all understanding, will guard your hearts and your minds in Christ Jesus. Finally, brothers, whatever is true, whatever is noble, whatever is right, whatever is pure, whatever is lovely, whatever is admirable—if anything is excellent or praiseworthy—think about such things. Whatever you have learned or received or heard from me, or seen in me—put it into practice. And the God of peace will be with you.

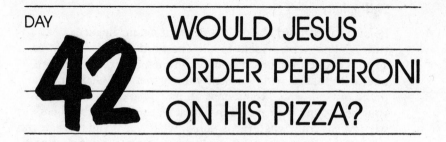

# WOULD JESUS ORDER PEPPERONI ON HIS PIZZA?

Would Jesus order pepperoni on His pizza?

Well, what do you think? Do you think He would? That's not one of life's more important questions, and your pastor is probably not going to preach on it next Sunday. But do you know what? There's something to that question that's worth finding out.

**Take a minute or two to read Luke 5:17–32.** This story shows two sides of Jesus. On one hand, Jesus had power from God to heal people and He did. On the other hand, He was *very human*, right down to eating dinner. But there's something more important here, and it's *who* Jesus ate dinner with. The Bible says that the pious Jews of the day (Pharisees) complained about who Jesus was eating with. These guys missed the whole point. They couldn't understand that Jesus was interested in giving such people—tax collectors, prostitutes, thieves—a new life.

Sometimes we get a picture of Jesus that is too one-sided. The simple (and mysterious) fact is that Jesus was human. He had friends, many who did not believe as He did. What does this mean to you?

First, it matters *who* your friends are. You can't go through life just hanging out with Christians, nor can you ever hope to be a consistent Christian if you have strong friendships with people who don't know God personally. Any adult who cautions you about your friends is right. The key is balance.

Second, be a person of conviction when you are with friends who don't know God. If they put you down, then your friendship isn't as important as you think.

Third, when you do things with your friends who don't know God, do safe things in neutral places. Their influence is stronger than you are, no matter what you think.

Friendships are important in life. Choose yours carefully and also be careful what you do with them. You'll save yourself a lot of hassles.

### Luke 5:29-32

Then Levi held a great banquet for Jesus at his house, and a large crowd of tax collectors and others were eating with them. But the Pharisees and the teachers of the law who belonged to their sect complained to his disciples, "Why do you eat and drink with tax collectors and 'sinners'?" Jesus answered them, "It is not the healthy who need a doctor, but the sick. I have not come to call the righteous, but sinners to repentance."

DAY **43** THE RIGHT COMMAND

If you've ever spent any time working on a computer terminal you know that in order to release a series of data commands you need one final release command. This becomes a key to everything you put in. The same thing is true in life. If we ever hope to have balance in the physical, social, and mental aspects of our lives, we will need the spiritual key to do it.

**Take some time and read Mark 12:28-34.** Jesus gave two commands here that can act as the spiritual keys we need:

—love God with all your heart, soul, mind, and strength
—love your neighbor as much as yourself

It's incredible, but wrapped up in these two phrases are the keys to a spiritually balanced life. Let's take a closer look:

1. The first phrase says love God with all your heart (emotions), soul (beliefs), mind (mentally), and strength (body). All the aspects we have been talking about—physical, mental, and now spiritual—are here. One key to being balanced spiritually is to bring all of you into the process of loving God. Take heart. God is not trying to turn you into a religious fanatic who can only eat, sleep, breathe, and talk religion. He sees you as a whole person not a "soul."

2. The second phrase says love your neighbor as yourself. Here is the social side of us. God expects us to spend time with all types of people and to show love for them all, including our families.

Spiritual balance will come in your life. Be patient with yourself and God. As you work to apply these commands and to stay balanced in the other areas of your life, God is committed to helping you in the process.

### Mark 12:28-31

One of the teachers of the law came and heard them debating. Noticing that Jesus had given them a good answer, he asked him, "Of all the commandments, which is the most important?" "The most important one," answered Jesus, "is this: 'Hear, O Israel, the Lord our God, the Lord is one. Love the Lord your God with all your heart and with all your soul and with all your mind and with all your strength.' The second is this: 'Love your neighbor as yourself.' There is no commandment greater than these."

"To get into our school, all you have to do is take the PSAT, the SAT, then come for an interview, and of course, your parents will have to . . ."

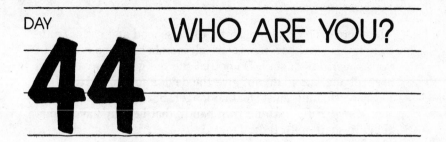

If a picture paints a thousand words
Then why can't I paint you;
No words could ever show,
The you I've come to know.

**DAVID GATES**

If you listen to Golden Oldies, you may have heard the words from the above song by Bread. It's a song about the masks people sometimes wear. To varying degrees, we all wear masks. We use them to hide behind, so that our real feelings and thoughts aren't seen. Masks are generally more bad than good. God's perfect plan is that you be free to be yourself—all the time. Unfortunately, sin has altered God's perfect plan, so we have to struggle with masks and hiding the truth. **Ephesians 4:17-32 has something helpful to say about masks. Take a few minutes and read it.**

Masks can come in many shapes. People try to act smarter, richer, or more popular than they really are. If you get turned down for a date but tell your friends it doesn't matter—that's wearing a mask. If you go out with your friends to do something that you feel inside is wrong—that's wearing a mask. Masks can hide our convictions, feelings, personalities, and Christianity from others. Are you lying to others by wearing a mask? The Bible says to stop lying to each other. Start today to be honest with yourself and others. You may need a little practice at first, especially if you've had some mask on for a while. Ask God to help you. The more honest you are with others about the real you, the more you will feel like a whole person.

### Ephesians 4:25–28

Therefore each of you must put off falsehood and speak truthfully to his neighbor, for we are all members of one body. "In your anger do not sin": Do not let the sun go down while you are still angry, and do not give the devil a foothold. He who has been stealing must steal no longer, but must work, doing something useful with his own hands, that he may have something to share with those in need.

# 45 WHAT KIND OF AN ANSWER IS THAT?

One of the myths of Christianity is that if you pray long or hard enough and are more holy, God will answer your prayers. You'll get the part-time job you need, the girl friend you want, a better relationship with your parents.

But is that really the truth? **Take several minutes to read the short book of Jonah.**

Almost everyone knows about how Jonah disobeyed God and was thrown into the sea and swallowed by a great fish. He knew he had to go to Nineveh as God told him to and tell the people that they would be destroyed because of their sin. It was not an easy thing to do. Often in our lives doing the right thing is not easy or comfortable.

Jonah must have felt good after the people turned from their sin. But when God had compassion and allowed them to live, Jonah got ticked. In fact, chapter 4 tells us that he felt so mad he wanted to die. Jonah didn't understand that God was trying to show him His kindness so that he would trust Him in all things. We don't know at the end of the story whether Jonah learned anything from his experience or not.

What about you? Are you willing to do what you know God wants you to, even when the results don't go your way? You may have to go the extra mile with your parents for a while without seeing them ease up on you. It may mean giving up friends who are bad influences on you without any friends in sight to take their place. In the long run it will always pay off to do what God's Word says. However, in the short run it helps to remember that walking with God doesn't mean we'll always be happy or comfortable. Ask God to help you today with your point of view.


### Jonah 3:1-5; 10

Then the word of the Lord came to Jonah a second time: "Go to the great city of Nineveh and proclaim to it the message I give you." Jonah obeyed the word of the Lord and went to Nineveh. Now Nineveh was a very large city; it took three days to go all through it. Jonah started into the city, going a day's journey, and he proclaimed: "Forty more days and Nineveh will be destroyed." The Ninevites believed God. They declared a fast, and all of them, from the greatest to the least, put on sackcloth. . . . When God saw what they did and how they turned from their evil ways, he had compassion and did not bring upon them the destruction he had threatened.

# 46 THE PROMISE

It used to be that few scientists would even consider that there is a God who created the universe and everything in it. But as man's ability to probe space grows, scientists are being forced to consider the possibility that God exists. Scientists have determined that everything in the universe is rushing away from everything else. If you ran time and the process backwards, then everything in the universe would be rushing faster and faster toward some central spot—some beginning. The conclusion? An Almighty God was there to start the whole process with the matter He Himself had created.

As Christians we sometimes get a one-sided view of God. Since we can never understand totally what He's about, the most we can do is look at who He is through ways He has interacted with people in the Bible, and how He has revealed Himself to us personally. But even then, it's hard to understand how He can judge our sin on one hand and be a loving Father on the other. Most of us know what it's like to be punished or judged, but few of us have really experienced pure unconditional love.

**Take a moment to read Romans 8:35–39.** This is some list of things that can't separate us from God's love, isn't it? Not life, not death, not angels, not the powers of hell, not your fears, not your worries, not even if you're flying or in a submarine.

Did you notice that "sin" is not included on the list? Sin separates us from God, but not from the love of God. If you feel alone or like you've failed again in a certain area, remember this promise—nothing can separate you from the love of God.

You can count on Him to forgive you and to be with you today and forever. This is a promise you can count on.

### Romans 8:35–39

Who shall separate us from the love of Christ? Shall trouble or hardship or persecution or famine or nakedness or danger or sword? As it is written:

> "For your sake we face death all day long;
> we are considered as sheep to be slaughtered."

No, in all these things we are more than conquerors through him who loved us. For I am convinced that neither death nor life, neither angels nor demons, neither the present nor the future, nor any powers, neither height nor depth, or anything else in all creation, will be able to separate us from the love of God that is in Christ Jesus our Lord.

# 47

# MOST POPULAR

How popular would you say you are? Not very? sort of? very? How did you get to be as popular or unpopular as you are? Having friends and their respect is important in life. But when collecting friends and their praise becomes too important, then your life goes out of balance.

Take a little time to read how popularity changed the way some people behaved. **Read John 12:37-50.**

In the case of the Jewish leaders in the story, respect and praise mattered more to them than what they believed. It mattered so much that they compromised their honesty.

Pushing for popularity can do the same thing to you. It's good to have friends, but whenever finding friends and looking for their praise takes your focus off important things in life, then things have gone too far.

In the same way, if you are already popular but to stay popular you have to compromise your Christian beliefs, then your life is out of balance. Balance is the key. And God can help you get it and maintain it. But the price of balance is not cheap. Check the balance in your life. Fewer activities, attending fewer parties, and learning to be comfortable alone sometimes may be in order.

Friendships and the respect of people are important. Having the friendship and respect of God is more important. Think about it.

### John 12:42–46

Yet at the same time many even among the leaders believed in him. But because of the Pharisees they would not confess their faith for fear they would be put out of the synagogue; for they loved praise from men more than praise from God. Then Jesus cried out, "When a man believes in me, he does not believe in me only, but in the one who sent me. When he looks at me, he sees the one who sent me. I have come into the world as a light, so that no one who believes in me should stay in darkness."

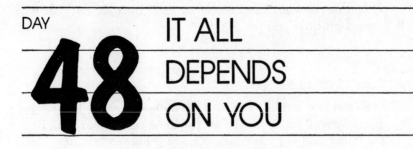

# IT ALL
# DEPENDS
# ON YOU

Some rather famous pictures came out of the late 1960s and early 1970s that said—without words—rebellion. A daisy stuck in the barrel of a policeman's rifle. A girl bent over a dead student at Kent State. A hippie with a middle finger pointing defiantly skyward. These images captured by the camera present not only an era in history, but also the rebellion in the heart of man.

Rebellion is in everyone. Even after you become a Christian, rebellion can still raise its head. How well do you handle rebellion? **Take some time and read a well-known story of a lost son, Luke 15:11–32.** Rebellion has consequences to be sure. The lost son spent his money, got quite hungry, and felt so low he went and took a job feeding pigs. But the story doesn't end there. The son made a choice to come back, not knowing exactly how his family would respond. His smart choice to live differently paid off.

And the choice to leave a rebellious spirit or attitude behind will pay off for you, too. God is not going to condemn you for wrestling with rebellion. However He is vitally concerned with how and if you channel it into something constructive.

Throughout your life you will have to learn to co-exist with rebellion. But as you let God control your life more and more, you will begin to see ways in which you can channel that desire for change into something useful. The church needs people who can channel their desire for change into new music, drama, strong leadership, and relevant thinking.

Rebellion in your life can be an asset or a liability. It will all depend on how you use it.

### Luke 15:21-24

"The son said to him, 'Father, I have sinned against heaven and against you. I am no longer worthy to be called your son.' But the father said to his servants, 'Quick! Bring the best robe and put it on him. Put a ring on his finger and sandals on his feet. Bring the fattened calf and kill it. Let's have a feast and celebrate. For this son of mine was dead and is alive again; he was lost and is found.' So they began to celebrate."

# 49 HIGH TECH

Stereos that clip onto your belt, TV's the size of a paper-back, telephones in cars and jets, and computer terminals in high school classrooms are strong clues that our world consumes and moves around large amounts of information. With all this information floating around, it can be tough to get a handle on what the truth is. Everyone seems to have an opinion about the right and wrong way to eat, pray, brush your teeth, or handle your kid brother. TV says one thing, teachers another. Friends and family only agree once in a while.

Over a thousand years ago a man named Paul wrote a let-ter to a young friend of his, Timothy, which talked about how to handle the information in our lives. **Take a moment to read 2 Timothy 3.**

These verses are really appropriate for our day. What is really interesting about this letter to Timothy is that it probably was one of the last letters Paul ever wrote. Just think. Paul used one of his last letters to a friend to tell him that God's Word is important and useful in helping us live our lives.

There is something for us to learn from this. God's Word is important in our lives. Without it, especially in today's infor-mation-packed world, we have little or no hope of making sense out of life. There's just too much out there to try to figure out.

How regularly are you reading God's Word? It's not how much you read or how long you think about it that counts. The chances of you keeping your head together are slim without regularly reading the Bible. God's Word can help you in life. If your Bible reading is irregular or only occasional you need to reevaluate just how important the Bible is to you. That doesn't mean you have to start reading every day. Set a reasonable goal for yourself so you read more this week than last. You'll find that God's Word can give you the help you need.

### 2 Timothy 3:12-15

In fact, everyone who wants to live a godly life in Christ Jesus will be persecuted, while evil men and impostors will go from bad to worse, deceiving and being deceived. But as for you, continue in what you have learned and have become convinced of, because you know those from whom you learned it, and how from infancy you have known the holy Scriptures, which are able to make you wise for salvation through faith in Christ Jesus.

# B-O-R-I-N-G

## 50

Is the Bible boring to you sometimes? Many Christians feel guilty and think something's wrong with their walk with God if the Bible doesn't speak to them all the time, every time. The *truth* is that it's normal to have times when the Bible reads like any other book. And let's face it, the Bible can be pretty tame stuff compared to what goes on TV or in the movies these days.

**For more insight on what to do when your Bible reading just isn't working, read Deuteronomy 6:1–9.** It's not very obvious at first, but here in this chapter is an angle on the problem of dry Bible reading. You'll notice God told the Jewish people to impress His commands on their children, to talk about them everywhere, to tie them to their hands (or memorize them), and write them on the door (communicate them to others). What was the point of all this? Two things are important.

**One:** God seems to be saying here that variety is good when it comes to learning His Word. There is no set way to have your devotions. If you are sharper in the morning, then read in the morning. If you want to read out loud to a friend or someone in your family, that's okay too. There is no law that says you have to read the Bible a certain way or at a certain time of the day. God encourages variety in reading His Word.

**Two:** There's an old saying that goes, "This Book [the Bible] will keep you from sin; sin will keep you from this Book." God's Word is valuable and can correct our bad thinking and instruct us on how to live a holy life in today's crazy world. But sin can keep us from getting the most from the Bible.

Next time your Bible reading gets boring, ask God to help

you. Check your life out. Then try some variety. If you are serious about being a Christian, you can't ignore God's Word. But with a little common sense, it can be your lifeline to God's best for your life.

### Deuteronomy 6:6–9

These commandments that I give you today are to be upon your hearts. Impress them on your children. Talk about them when you sit at home and when you walk along the road, when you lie down and when you get up. Tie them as symbols on your hands and bind them on your foreheads. Write them on the doorframes of your houses and on your gates.

"I've been studying for two hours. Why do you ask, Mom?"

Trying to do two things at once in life can have rather serious complications. Study for a test and watch David Letterman, and you'll laugh a lot but probably flunk your test. Impress your friends with how fast your 1962 BMW goes as you drive across town, and you'll most likely wind up with an invitation to pay the police some money. Certain things just do not mix in life. The Bible talks about two attitudes that don't mix. **Read about them for the next few minutes in James 4:1–17.**

The Bible is clear—being friends with the evil pleasures of the world makes you an enemy of God. This is not easy or fun to hear. But it is very, very true.

Some of the most unhappy and frustrated Christians are those who try to party on Friday and Saturday night and then show up for church on Sunday morning. It just doesn't work. Christianity requires our concentrated commitment. It is not designed for people who are undecided about its value. Now this doesn't mean we have to become reclusive and hide away from the world. It doesn't mean that life has to become one long prayer meeting either. What it *does* mean is that the value system of a Christian is different. Having a good time, dressing well, and partying with lots of friends have their place in a Christian's life but—and get this—not the *same* place as in the life of someone who doesn't know the Lord. The Christian's motivation, attitude, and actions are going in a different direction than those of the world. This is especially true when it comes to pleasure.

Are you trying to have a good time God's way *and* the world's way? It won't work. Put your whole commitment into doing things God's way, and you'll see some of the pieces of your life start to fit together.

### James 4:1-4

What causes fights and quarrels among you? Don't they come from your desires that battle within you? You want something but don't get it. You kill and covet, but you cannot have what you want. You quarrel and fight. You do not have, because you do not ask God. When you ask, you do not receive, because you ask with wrong motives, that you may spend what you get on your pleasures. You adulterous people, don't you know that friendship with the world is hatred toward God? Anyone who chooses to be a friend of the world becomes an enemy of God.

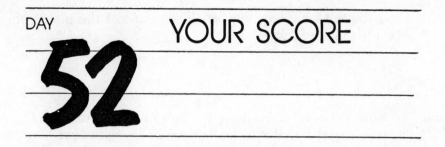

# YOUR SCORE

How would you rate your batting average when it comes to temptation? Would you say you are winning more than you're losing? Losing more battles than you're winning? Maybe things have gotten gray, and if you were honest with yourself you haven't been tempted for some time. Sometimes temptation is very clear. Shoplifting or having sex or damaging others' property are easy to spot as wrong. Other times, right and wrong aren't so clearly defined. How do you handle temptation when it comes? **Take a moment and read 1 Corinthians 10:1-14.**

Sometimes God doesn't have to discipline us for sin—we discipline and even punish ourselves. At the time, it's easier to give in and do what we want, but we usually pay for it. Embarrassment, guilt, hurt, broken relationships, even death can result when we give in to temptation.

When Jesus died on the cross, He broke the *power* of sin in your life. How this works is still a mystery to man. The important thing to remember is that while the *power* of sin in your life was broken by Jesus' dying, you will still sin. No man will ever die having completely beaten sin in his life. This doesn't mean we should give up and give in to temptation. What it *does* mean is that God wants to help us get our batting averages up and give in to temptation less and less.

Ask God to help you hear His voice clearly when you are being tempted. Now you may not hear a real voice, but God can guide your thoughts and conscience so that you will find the way of escape He promised.

### *1 Corinthians 10:13, 14*

No temptation has seized you except what is common to man. And God is faithful; he will not let you be tempted beyond what you can bear. But when you are tempted, he will also provide a way out so that you can stand up under it. Therefore, my dear friends, flee from idolatry.

# "IT'LL GO ON YOUR RECORD"

"It'll go on your record." If you had a dollar for every time you've heard that one, you could buy a one-way ticket to China for your plane geometry teacher. Just where are these records kept anyway? (Probably in some vault in Kentucky along with stacks of confederate dollars.)

As a Christian, God keeps records on you. **To find out exactly what He records, take some time to read Psalms 103 and Luke 10:20.**

The verses in Psalms tell you what God *doesn't* put on your record—your sins. The Bible says God doesn't bear a grudge or remain angry forever; and that He has moved our sin away from us, as far as east is from west—in other words, a distance which defies measurement. You may have noticed that God moves the sin away from *you.* Why? Because God loves you as a person but hates the sin in your life. Separating you from your sin by more miles than you can measure guarantees God will never see you and your sin together. It guarantees that we are forgiven— thoroughly. The one record that *is* kept on you is whether your name is registered as a citizen of heaven. Sometimes concepts like this (whether your name is written down in glory) seem off-the-wall, particularly in our world which is so in tune with what can be seen and experienced. But do you know what? The concept *is* real. Your whole hope of living after you die is tied to this concept. The Bible has made it clear that when people come to Christ for forgiveness of sins their names *are* recorded in heaven.

Do you have a sense of peace in your life that a record of

your name has been established with God? Maybe you've been faking your Christianity for so long that you've fooled even yourself. Knowing God personally is your only hope for a meaningful life and living forever. Or maybe you've got sin in your life and you need to talk with God. He's waiting to hear from you. Take some time today, right now, to set the record straight with Him.

*Psalms 103:11–14*

For as high as the heavens are above the earth, so great is his love for those who fear him; as far as the east is from the west, so far has he removed our transgressions from us. As a father has compassion on his children, so the Lord has compassion on those who fear him; for he knows how we are formed, he remembers that we are dust.

*Luke 10:20*

"However, do not rejoice that the spirits submit to you, but rejoice that your names are written in heaven."

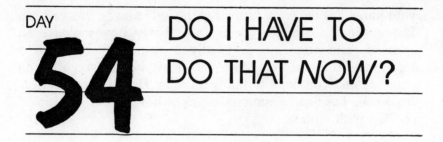

You would think with all the moaning and groaning young people do about chores that parents would give up their silly ideas and just take out the trash, cut the grass, and do the dishes themselves. But no way! Parents can be tough cookies when it comes to chores, and it will be a cold day in July in Texas before they'll ever give up their notion that *you* should help around the house!

Chores are a part of living. Always have been. Always will be. How is your attitude about chores? **Take a minute and read what the Bible says about attitude. Read 1 Peter 3:10-17.**

These verses give you a formula for a happy attitude toward life:

—Keep control of your tongue. (Do your chores without complaining.)
—Don't tell lies. (Are they *really* done?)
—Turn away from evil. (Be honest. Do them when you are told to.)
—Live in peace, even if you have to chase it. (Accept the criticism and the praise when it comes.)

It takes a lot of energy to keep a house going and in order. Sometimes parents can get so busy that they assign you chores without thinking about your tests or date. The same formula that will help you handle the chores will also help you work out the differences with your folks. By sitting down and being reasonable with your folks (controlling your tongue, and doing your best to keep peace) about the problem, you will demonstrate an attitude that is pleasing to your parents and to God.

### 1 Peter 3:10–12

For, "Whoever would love life and see good days must keep his tongue from evil and his lips from deceitful speech. He must turn from evil and do good; he must seek peace and pursue it. For the eyes of the Lord are on the righteous and his ears are attentive to their prayer, but the face of the Lord is against those who do evil."

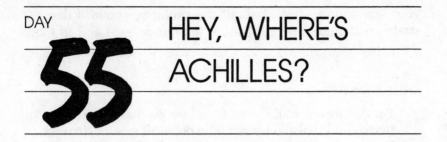

# HEY, WHERE'S ACHILLES?

The Achilles tendon in your lower leg gets its name from the Greek soldier who, supposedly immune to enemy wounds except in his lower leg tendon, died when an arrow hit him in—you guessed it—the Achilles tendon. If you ever pulled that tendon in sports you know it can be a painful injury.

We have Achilles tendons in other areas of our lives, too. For some reason everyone's personality is predisposed to a besetting sin or repeated failure in one area of his or her life. How do we deal with our Achilles tendons? **Read Romans 7:15-25 for some insight into this.**

Sometimes we get the impression that men in the Bible like Paul were spiritual giants who didn't struggle in life as we do. These verses should put that myth in order, since Paul gets down to some honest, gut-level communication. Whatever it was, Paul's Achilles tendon went with him. Paul, like many people who know the Lord, wanted to please God with a holy life, but found himself sometimes beaten by some sin in his life.

As long as we live, we still struggle with sin. When you're younger, sex will be a regular and troublesome temptation. And as you get older what tempts you might change.

The *power* of sin in your life was broken when Christ died on the cross. But even though the power of sin is broken in your life, you will still sin. Like Paul we have to turn to Christ to rescue us.

As a Christian, sin no longer should control you. Use your head and stay out of situations where you are easily tempted. Call on God often for help. Doing these things will help you win not only the war, but more battles along the way, too.

### Romans 7:15-20

I do not understand what I do. For what I want to do I do not do, but what I hate I do. And if I do what I do not want to do, I agree that the law is good. As it is, it is no longer I myself who do it, but it is sin living in me. I know that nothing good lives in me, that is, in my sinful nature. For I have the desire to do what is good, but I cannot carry it out. For what I do is not the good I want to do; no, the evil I do not want to do—this I keep on doing. Now if I do what I do not want to do, it is no longer I who do it, but it is sin living in me that does it.

FOL

3 2024